WONDERFUL NATURAL WONDERS

NIAGARA FALLS

BY BRAY JACOBSON

Gareth Stevens PUBLISHING

Please visit our website, www.garethstevens.com. For a free color catalog of all our high-quality books, call toll free 1-800-542-2595 or fax 1-877-542-2596.

Library of Congress Cataloging-in-Publication Data

Names: Jacobson, Bray, author.
Title: Niagara Falls / Bray Jacobson.
Description: New York : Gareth Stevens Publishing, 2023. | Series: Wonderful natural wonders | Includes index.
Identifiers: LCCN 2021036567 (print) | LCCN 2021036568 (ebook) | ISBN 9781538276860 (set) | ISBN 9781538276877 (library binding) | ISBN 9781538276853 (paperback) | ISBN 9781538276884 (ebook)
Subjects: LCSH: Niagara Falls (N.Y. and Ont.)–Juvenile literature.
Classification: LCC F127.N8 J34 2023 (print) | LCC F127.N8 (ebook) | DDC 971.3/39–dc23
LC record available at https://lccn.loc.gov/2021036567
LC ebook record available at https://lccn.loc.gov/2021036568

Published in 2023 by
Gareth Stevens Publishing
29 E. 21st Street
New York, NY 10010

Designer: Tanya Dellaccio
Editor: Kristen Nelson

Photo credits: Cover skostep/Shutterstock.com; background texture (pp 3-24) BEMPhoto_31/ Shutterstock.com; p. 5 Serjio74/Shutterstock.com; p. 7 Rainer Lesniewski/Shutterstock.com; p. 9 Olesya Baron/Shutterstock.com; p. 11 YingHui Liu/Shutterstock.com; p. 13 Derek Robertson/Shutterstock.com; p. 15 Nicholas Jungman/Shutterstock.com; p. 17 JArmando e ClauEleone/Shutterstock.com; p. 19 Rod Adolfo/Shutterstock.com; p. 21 Vadim Rodnev/Shutterstock.com.

Printed in the United States of America

CPSIA compliance information: Batch #CSGS23: For further information contact Gareth Stevens, New York, New York at 1-800-542-2595.

CONTENTS

Boldface words appear in the glossary.

Watch the Water Fall

Waterfalls are some of the most beautiful natural sights on Earth! When a body of water flows over a **steep** ledge into a pool below, that's a waterfall. Niagara Falls is a waterfall often called a natural wonder.

Where Is It?

Niagara Falls is on the Niagara River. The river runs between Lake Erie and Lake Ontario. It separates the U.S. state of New York and the Canadian **province** of Ontario. The United States and Canada share care and **management** of Niagara Falls.

ONTARIO
LAKE ONTARIO
U.S-CANADA BORDER
NIAGARA FALLS
NIAGARA RIVER
NEW YORK
LAKE ERIE

Three Falls

Niagara Falls is made up of three waterfalls. The largest is Horseshoe Falls, named because it curves. It falls on the Canadian side of the **border**. It's more than 160 feet (49 m) tall and about 2,600 feet (790 m) wide along its curve.

HORSESHOE FALLS

The American Falls is on the U.S. side of the border. It's about 110 feet (34 m) at its tallest. It's about 850 feet (260 m) wide. At its tallest, Bridal Veil Falls is 120 feet (37 m). It's only about 45 feet (14 m) wide.

BRIDAL VEIL FALLS
AMERICAN FALLS

Forming the Falls

Niagara Falls is thousands of years old! First, a **glacier** formed the **Great Lakes**. Their **drainage** created the Niagara River. The water flowed downward because Lake Erie is at a higher elevation than Lake Ontario.

The water wore away rock and a waterfall formed. Over time, **erosion** of softer rock created the steep drops of today's falls. Erosion still occurs at Niagara Falls! About 1 foot (0.3 m) of rock is worn away each year.

Water Power

Niagara Falls is an amazing sight because of the amount of water that flows over the falls. This water comes from the drainage of four of the Great Lakes. At most, 6 million cubic feet (168,000 cu m) of water run over the falls every minute!

Hydroelectric power is electricity created by moving water. The very first hydroelectric power plant used the waters of the Niagara. It opened in 1895. Today, the United States and Canada both use Niagara Falls to create power.

Falls Parks

In both the United States and Canada, Niagara Falls and the area around it are **protected** as parks. Millions of people from around the world visit the awesome natural wonder each year. They take in the sights and even take boat rides near the falls!

GLOSSARY

border: a line separating one country or state from another

drainage: the process of removing liquid from somewhere by letting it flow out

elevation: height above sea level

erosion: the act of wearing away by water, wind, or ice

glacier: a large area of ice that moves slowly over an area of land

Great Lakes: a group of lakes in North America that all connect. They are Huron, Ontario, Michigan, Erie, and Superior.

management: the act or process of deciding how to use something

protect: to keep safe

province: an area of a country

steep: almost straight up and down

FOR MORE INFORMATION

BOOKS

Simons, Lisa M. B. *Niagara Falls.* Lake Elmo, MN: Focus Readers, 2018.

Troup, Roxanne. *Amazing Waterfalls Around the World.* North Mankato, MN: Capstone Press, 2019.

WEBSITES

Niagara Falls State Park
www.niagarafallsstatepark.com
Do you want to visit Niagara Falls? Check out the state park website to plan your trip!

Pictures of Waterfalls Around the World
www.nationalgeographic.com/travel/article/pictures-waterfalls-around-world
Waterfalls are amazing! See more here.

Publisher's note to educators and parents: Our editors have carefully reviewed these websites to ensure that they are suitable for students. Many websites change frequently, however, and we cannot guarantee that a site's future contents will continue to meet our high standards of quality and educational value. Be advised that students should be closely supervised whenever they access the internet.

INDEX